TERROR AT THE
MUNICH OLYMPICS

Essential Events

TERROR AT THE
MUNICH OLYMPICS

BY COURTNEY FARRELL

Content Consultants
Eric Mogren, PhD, Associate Professor of History
Northern Illinois University

Bernard Reich, PhD, Professor of Political Science and International Affairs
The George Washington University

ABDO
Publishing Company

CREDITS

Published by ABDO Publishing Company, 8000 West 78th Street, Edina, Minnesota 55439. Copyright © 2010 by Abdo Consulting Group, Inc. International copyrights reserved in all countries. No part of this book may be reproduced in any form without written permission from the publisher. The Essential Library™ is a trademark and logo of ABDO Publishing Company.

Printed in the United States of America,
North Mankato, Minnesota
102009
012010

 PRINTED ON RECYCLED PAPER

Editor: Chrös McDougall
Copy Editor: Paula Lewis
Interior Design and Production: Nicole Brecke
Cover Design: Nicole Brecke

Library of Congress Cataloging-in-Publication Data
Farrell, Courtney.
 Terror at the Munich Olympics / Courtney Farrell.
    p. cm. — (Essential events)
 Includes bibliographical references and index.
 ISBN 978-1-60453-945-5
 1. Olympic Games (20th : 1972 : Munich, Germany)—Juvenile literature. 2. Terrorism—Germany—Munich—History—Juvenile literature. I. Title.
 GV7221972 .F37 2010
 796.48—dc22

                              2009030426

TABLE OF CONTENTS

The Israeli delegation paraded into Olympic Stadium in Munich, West Germany, during the opening ceremonies for the 1972 Olympics.

"THE GAMES OF PEACE AND JOY"

he planners of the 1972 Munich Olympics wanted to show the world a changed country, an open and democratic West Germany. The last time Germany hosted an Olympics was the 1936 Berlin Games, when Nazi restrictions had banned many Jewish athletes from competing. At that time, Adolf Hitler was orchestrating the Holocaust, which, by its end, resulted in the murders of some 6 million Jews.

The painful memories of that event were still fresh in the minds of Jewish people and others around the world in 1972. Now, almost four decades later, West Germany wanted to show that it was an open and peaceful country. The Germans invited the press in record numbers to witness what was dubbed "The Games of Peace and Joy." Even the Olympic security guards fit the friendly new image. They strolled the Olympic parks unarmed, looking distinctly nonmilitary in sky-blue uniforms. But all was not as peaceful as it appeared.

During the second week of competition, on the morning of September 5, eight young Palestinian terrorists began their attack. The men, members of the Black September terrorist organization, approached the Olympic Village, which housed the athletes. Security there was poor. The gate to the Olympic Village was locked at night, but athletes coming back from late-night parties routinely climbed over the fence to return to their rooms.

The terrorists were dressed in tracksuits. They looked like Olympic competitors as they slipped inside the Olympic Village. They had already chosen their target: the building where the Israeli delegation slept. Their goal was to gain world attention for their cause—opposition to existence of the State of Israel. Armed with grenades and machine guns, the terrorists invaded the building. They took 11 members of the Israeli delegation hostage. Two were soon killed.

After a 20-hour standoff with German security

The Nazi Olympics

Adolf Hitler believed that the Aryan (white) race was superior to all others, and he hoped to use the 1936 Berlin Olympics to prove his theory to the world. His was not going to be a fair test, however, since he denied spots on the German Olympic team to Jewish athletes—including those capable of winning gold medals.

Preparations for the Berlin Olympics included removal of "No Jews" signs in public places to give visitors a favorable view of Germany. But swastikas, the Nazi Party's official emblem, were everywhere. Weeks before the games, Hitler ordered Gypsies to be rounded up and imprisoned in concentration camps so they would not be seen on the streets. The Germans saw Gypsies as having mixed blood and being dangerous.

The 18 black athletes on the U.S. team proved that Hitler's Aryan superiority idea was false. They won 14 medals, nearly a quarter of the U.S. total for the Olympic Games. Jesse Owens was a track-and-field star who broke three world records. German athlete Carl Ludwig "Luz" Long warmly congratulated Owens immediately after Owens defeated him. "It took a lot of courage for him to befriend me in front of Hitler," Owens remembered.[1]

forces and police, the remaining nine Israelis and five of the Palestinians lay dead. The tragic events at the Munich Olympics brought terrorism and Arab-Israeli conflict to the world stage.

The Roots of the Arab-Israeli Conflict

At its heart, the Arab-Israeli conflict is a dispute over land between the Palestinian Arabs and the Jews. More than 2,000 years ago, the small strip of land in the Middle East that is now the nation of Israel was for centuries home to a Jewish kingdom. In 586 BCE, many Jews were pushed out of the area. They spent the next several centuries without a true home and were persecuted wherever they went.

The modern conflict originated in the nineteenth century. After years of persecution, large numbers of Jews began moving back to their ancient homeland. However, there was a problem. Much of the area that was once their homeland was now called Palestine. Most of the inhabitants were Arabs whose ancestors had lived there at least 1,000 years. Religious differences inflamed the situation further. Jews, Muslims, and Christians occupied the land, and each religion considered it to be sacred.

Islam

People who practice Islam are called Muslims. Just as Christians and Jews do, believers worship one god, but they revere Muhammad as God's prophet. The Koran, the sacred text of Islam, teaches Muslims to treat each other as brothers and sisters, donate to charity, fast, pray regularly, and make a pilgrimage to Mecca. One aspect of Islam that concerns non-Muslims is *jihad*, or struggle. This can also be seen as "holy war." In the contemporary world, some terrorists have adopted the term to legitimize the violence they commit against "idolaters" in the name of God. Some governments have also declared a holy war, or jihad, against their enemies. Most of the world's Muslims denounce this interpretation of jihad.

The conflict worsened after World War I (1914–1918). Palestine had been in the Ottoman Empire, which was defeated in the war. Afterward, the League of Nations divided the former Ottoman lands between the victorious Allies. In 1917, the British took control of Palestine. They were instructed to develop the country into a national home for the Jewish people. This caused conflict between the Arab Palestinians and the new Jewish immigrants. The result was fighting and terrorism.

The fighting continued in 1948 when the State of Israel became independent. Its independence continues today. The Israeli Jews, Arab Muslims, and Christians each believe they should control the land, and they have not found a compromise. Some Arabs would like to eliminate Israel altogether. The Black September terrorists were among those. The Munich

One of the Black September terrorists looking off the balcony from the apartment where the Israeli athletes were being held hostage

kidnapping brought worldwide attention to the Palestinians' cause and was one of the most visible examples of terrorism between the two peoples.

What Is Terrorism?

Terrorists use violence and target noncombatants in an attempt to influence events, change policy, or make a political statement. Acts of violence are often followed by statements claiming responsibility and making demands. These attacks are usually well publicized and would lose much of their effectiveness if they were unseen.

Terrorism is a tool of small groups battling against larger, more powerful rivals. Unexpected violence is intended to spread terror throughout the target population. As public anxiety increases, even the possibility of an attack can wield power. Delays at security checkpoints, for example, remind citizens of the threat. Terrorists hope that frightened populations will give in to demands, but this does not usually work. Most governments have a policy to never negotiate with terrorists. Giving in to terrorist demands only encourages other extremists to carry out their own attacks.

Suicide Bombers

In the Palestinian society, families of suicide bombers are honored. Many receive cash payments from donors—often, wealthy Saudis or others—who support their *jihad*. The bombers are considered heroes and brave martyrs in the struggle against the enemy. Suicide bombers are extremely difficult to detect since explosives can be concealed under clothing and detonated in crowded places.

Who Are Terrorists?

Why would a person decide to become a terrorist and risk death or imprisonment? Psychologists have tried to answer this question in the hope of ending the violent practice.

Terrorists fight for "cause and comrades."[2] Their ideology and their loyalty to their group must become more important to them than life itself. Some terrorists were born into conflict. For example, some Palestinian children are born in refugee camps and are taught to hate Israelis. Other terrorists are not involved with extremist groups until later in life, when they take on the group's cause as their own.

Being part of a small, secretive group with a grandiose mission provides members with a strong sense of belonging. Lonely or insecure people often are recruited into these groups. The groups provide friends, financial support, and excitement. Terrorist cells generally pressure members to drop their associations with families and friends. This helps increase the group's influence over the individual. People with traumatic personal histories are especially susceptible to domination by a charismatic group leader. They might

Religious Extremists

Religious terrorist groups pose a great security concern because of their disregard for both the lives of others and their own lives. Generally, religious terrorists believe that God sanctions their acts of violence and they expect to be rewarded in the afterlife. Followers believe that by dying for their cause, they will be martyred and that such a death is a sure path to heaven.

even be induced to sacrifice their lives through a suicide mission.

The Black September terrorists in Munich succeeded in gaining attention for their cause. However, terrorism continues today and still has not brought the Israelis or the Palestinians the result that they are ultimately seeking. ⌐

Hamas

Hamas is a radical terrorist and militant Palestinian political organization that has carried out many terrorist attacks and suicide bombings against Israel. Hamas is committed to Israel's destruction. However, it also provides social services to the Palestinian people, including schools, health care clinics, and orphanages.

The group was founded in 1987 and seeks to eliminate Israel and establish a Muslim state in its place. In 2006, Hamas won a majority in the Palestinian parliament. It continues to launch attacks into Israel. Since 1993, Hamas is said to have launched more than 350 terrorist attacks against Israel that have killed more than 500 people.

*U.S. Air Force officers carrying the coffin of murdered
Israeli Olympic weight lifter David Berger*

The Temple Mount, or Noble Sanctuary, is revered by Jews and Muslims, but for different reasons.

ANCIENT ROOTS
OF A MODERN WAR

The first Hebrew tribes were Jews who likely moved into Canaan, now Israel, between 1800 and 1500 BCE. Many different peoples controlled the land after that, including the Jews. It was not until around the seventh century CE that

Islam originated and Muslims began moving there. The Arab Muslims took control of the area when they defeated the Byzantines in 638 CE.

The land largely remained under some Muslim control until the twentieth century, although a small number of Jews never left. In 1516, the area became part of the Muslim Ottoman Empire. Jews were slowly welcomed back during Ottoman rule to escape persecution in other parts of the world and for religious reasons. But the population remained mostly Arab Muslims. That began to change during the nineteenth century. Jewish immigration began to increase in the 1880s and continued into the twentieth century. The Ottoman Empire lost control of the area in 1918, after World War I. By 1948, Jews had declared the independent State of Israel.

Oppression of Jews in History

The Jews have spent much of their existence without their own state. According to Jewish belief, centuries after arriving in Canaan, a famine forced many Jews to move into Egypt around 1522 BCE. They were welcomed at first, but eventually the Egyptians began to enslave the Jews. After wandering for 40 years, the Jews returned to Canaan between 1250 and 1210 BCE. Throughout the next seven centuries, the Israelite kingdom was founded, unified, and split in two. During those years, the Jews built the first Holy Temple in Jerusalem, making it the center of Judaism.

Then, in approximately 586 BCE, the Babylonians destroyed the Holy Temple and drove the Jews out of the area, then called Judah. Approximately 50 years later, when the Persians took over, some Jews were allowed to return and rebuild the Holy Temple.

In 167 BCE, the Jews created a new, independent state called Judah. But

A Holy Land

Jews, Muslims, and Christians revere many holy sites in Jerusalem, the capital of Israel. That is why many people of those religions yearn to live there. Unfortunately, that can also lead to disputes.

According to Jewish tradition, God ordered the Jewish patriarch Abraham to sacrifice his son Isaac in Jerusalem. Many years later, in 957 BCE, King Solomon of the ancient Israelites built the first Jewish Holy Temple. The temple was built at the location of Isaac's sacrifice. The Jews call this area the Temple Mount. Today, only the Western Wall from a second Holy Temple remains. But many Jews consider this to be the holiest site in Judaism.

The third holiest site in Islam is also in Jerusalem. According to Muslim tradition, the prophet Muhammad ascended to heaven at *al-Haram al-Sharif*, or the Noble Sanctuary. The Muslims later built a shrine there called the Dome of the Rock as well as the al-Aqsa Mosque. There was a problem, however. The site was the same as Temple Mount.

People of both religions consider this area to be one of the most sacred sites in the world, but for different reasons. Control of this holy area remains one of the key disagreements between the Israeli Jews and the Arab Muslims today.

in 63 BCE, the Romans took control
of Judah. The Jews revolted and
briefly took control back in 66 CE.
But in 70 CE, the Romans took the
land back and destroyed all but the
Western Wall of the temple. Jews
would not control the land again
until 1948.

In 132 CE, when the Romans did
not let the Jews rebuild the Holy
Temple for a third time, the Jews
revolted. The Romans destroyed the Jewish state.
Most Jews moved to other areas in the Middle East,
Africa, and Europe, where they were not accepted.
Although some Jews stayed in Palestine, most lived
elsewhere for the next several centuries.

A Third Temple?

Some Jews would like to
rebuild the Holy Temple
that the Romans destroyed
nearly 2,000 years ago.
There is a major problem.
The Islamic Dome of the
Rock was built on the same
location as the original
two temples. The Temple
Mount/Noble Sanctuary is
now one of the most con-
tested pieces of land in the
world.

The Jews faced discrimination, or anti-
Semitism, in nearly all countries they settled in,
which ranged from social exclusion to murder. The
persecution increased dramatically with the rise
of Christianity. One prominent example was the
Spanish Inquisition. Some historians believe more
than 150,000 Jews were killed during this period
from approximately 1478 to 1834 because their
beliefs differed from those of the Catholic Church.

Theodor Herzl

In 1887, Theodor Herzl organized the first Zionist Congress in Basel, Switzerland. The congress brought the Zionist movement together and created a united Zionist political platform for the first time. The platform, which called for a Jewish state in Palestine and rejected other options for a Jewish home, was not immediately popular. Herzl, an Austrian journalist, argued that the only way Jews could be secure was if they had their own state. He is now considered the father of modern Zionism.

In the 20th century, approximately 6 million Jews were killed during the Holocaust.

Even though most Jews did not live in what is now Israel for many centuries, they still consider the area to be their homeland.

The Zionist Movement

Despite their frequent relocation, Jews maintained their culture and religion, and many never stopped considering Jerusalem to be their true home. Zionism is the Jewish people's desire to have their own state in their ancient homeland. This desire is biblical in origin, but it took on new meaning during the nineteenth century with the rise of Political Zionism.

Over time, as anti-Semitism increased in Europe, so did waves of Jewish immigration to Palestine. By the nineteenth century, many Jews, including the "Father of Zionism," Theodor Herzl, believed the only way to avoid persecution was to have their own state. The Political Zionists believed this state needed to be in Palestine.

In 1880, it is estimated that fewer than
25,000 Jews lived in Palestine. After two waves of
immigration, the first beginning in the 1880s and
the second beginning in 1914, an estimated 85,000
Jews were living in Palestine. This trend would
continue as anti-Semitism grew throughout Europe,
but not without opposition from the native Arabs.

The Mandate Period

The Zionists received a boost when the British
issued the Balfour Declaration in 1917. In that,
Britain expressed its support for the creation of a
Jewish national home in Palestine. The League of
Nations officially approved the terms of the Balfour
Declaration in the 1922 Mandate for Palestine.
The violence that followed the declaration did not
dissuade Jews from continuing to immigrate to
the area.

Both Jews and Arabs believed the mandate
granted them the right to control all of the land.
Instead, the British controlled the land and did
not set clear standards for immigration and land
purchases. The Arabs were upset that large numbers
of Jews were immigrating and buying land. They
feared the Jews would take control of the land.

These tensions often resulted in violence. Some of
the violence was among the Jews and Arabs. The Jews
also began attacking the British once new British laws
restricted Jewish immigration after World War II.

THE HOLOCAUST

Worldwide support for the Zionist movement
increased following the Holocaust. Starting in 1933,
shortly after Hitler became chancellor of Germany,
the German Nazi Party made it their official goal to
eliminate the Jews. The Holocaust resulted in the
organized extermination of approximately 6 million
Jews and severe oppression of many more.

The Holocaust came to an end with the Allied
victory in World War II on May 8, 1945. After years
of discrimination in Europe, the Holocaust was the
final straw for many Jews. Some had already fled to
Palestine to avoid Nazi persecution in the 1940s.
After the war, an influx of Holocaust survivors
arrived in Palestine eager to create a new Jewish state.
But, Arab Palestinians already occupied the land.
Their ancestors had lived there for hundreds of
years. The conflict over land was about to intensify.

Jewish youths headed to the British Mandate of Palestine after being released from Buchenwald concentration camp in Germany in 1945.

*Israeli Prime Minister David Ben-Gurion looked on as an official held up
the document proclaiming the creation of Israel on May 14, 1948.*

ISRAELI STATEHOOD

s the influx of Jews into Palestine
increased throughout the early 1900s,
so did the tension between the Jews and the Arabs.
Meanwhile, the Jews were also unhappy with the

British, whose laws limited immigration and land purchases. The Jews often attacked the British troops. After years of fending off Jewish and Arab attacks, the British left Palestine in 1947 and called on the United Nations (UN) to help. The UN tried to solve the conflict that November by dividing Palestine into a Jewish state and an Arab state and turning Jerusalem into an internationally controlled city. Although the Jews agreed to this plan, it died when the Arabs rejected it. By 1948, recurring raids and skirmishes grew into a full Arab-Israeli war.

On May 14, 1948, the Jewish State of Israel was founded. The United States and the Soviet Union officially recognized the new state within days, giving the country legitimacy on the world stage. But the Arab world was infuriated. Palestinians enlisted the support of troops from Egypt, Syria, Iraq, and Transjordan to attack Israel just days later. The Israelis won the battle, assuring their new nation's existence. However, the peace and security that the Jews sought in creating Israel would have to wait.

ISRAEL TAKES OVER, PALESTINE SUFFERS

The two Palestinian areas not taken by the Israelis were what are now called the West Bank and the

Gaza Strip. The West Bank, a 2,263-square-mile (5861-sq-km) piece of land between Israel and Jordan, was annexed as part of Jordan. Egypt took control of the Gaza Strip, the 141-square-mile (365-sq-km) area bordering Israel, Egypt, and the Mediterranean Sea. But the fighting displaced more than 700,000 Palestinians from Israel. In events that are still disputed, they fled or were driven from their homes. Most never returned.

A Population Explosion

A population explosion among Palestinian refugees has also made returning to their land difficult.

Palestinian birthrates are among the highest in the world. Overpopulation intensifies stress and strains the limited resources. Today, there is severe crowding in Gaza. In Jabalia, a densely populated camp near Gaza City, approximately 106,856 refugees live on .54 square miles (1.4 sq km) of land.

The majority of displaced Palestinians ended up in refugee camps in Jordan, Lebanon, Syria, and Gaza. Conditions in the camps were horrific. There was never enough food, and the rocky land could not be farmed. People lived in tents that sweltered in the summer and froze in winter. They became dependent upon UN food aid just to survive. As the people in the camps suffered, Palestinian resentment toward Israel grew.

Refugee camps once filled with tents grew into huge slums with long stretches of dilapidated buildings.

Palestinians stood outside tents after their homes were destroyed by Israeli rockets in 2009.

Meanwhile, stories of the beauty of their lost land passed from one generation of Palestinian refugees to the next. Hatred of Israelis festered, allowing radical militias many opportunities for attracting new recruits. All of the terrorists who attacked the Israelis at the 1972 Munich Olympics were born and raised in Palestinian refugee camps.

These refugee camps have improved over the
years, but they still remain overcrowded and in need
of massive infrastructure improvements and outside
aid. The camps
have become a
breeding ground
for new terrorists.

THE PALESTINIAN POINT OF VIEW

Palestinians
see themselves as
an indigenous
population
driven from
their homeland
by invaders.
Palestinians wonder
how the Jews,
who were once
themselves without
a homeland, could
shift that fate to
them. When asked
where they come

Inside the Refugee Camps Today

The United Nations Relief and Works Agency refugee camps are located in areas surrounding Israel proper, including Jordan, Lebanon, Syria, the West Bank, and the Gaza Strip. These camps began as tent villages in the late 1940s but have grown into huge slums. Small camps include residents numbering in the hundreds, but camps of 40,000 to 90,000 people are common. The residents do not own the land they live on, so they are not motivated to make long-term improvements to it, and most cannot afford to do so.

Little greenery survives inside the camps. Shacks made of concrete blocks line dusty roads. Approximately 20 extended family members crowd into each small home. The cement shacks were built as temporary shelters in the 1960s, and they have not held up well.

The United Nations provides health care, distributes food, and maintains schools. Still, living conditions are terrible. Electricity is sporadic, and roads and sewers are not maintained. Open sewers crisscross through some of the camps. The sewers flood when it rains, which poses a health hazard. Children are especially vulnerable to intestinal parasites and other illnesses common in such conditions.

from, Palestinian refugee children name their ancestral villages that are now in Israel. The majority of them have never been to these villages, but they have been taught to consider the area home.

THE JEWISH POINT OF VIEW

Jews argue that they are the rightful inhabitants of the land. Their claim to the land extends back to 1800–1500 BCE, when the first Hebrew, or Jewish, tribes settled the area. After that, their social, political, and religious center remained in Jerusalem until the diaspora following the Jewish revolt in 132 CE.

Israelis have also pointed to the Balfour Declaration of 1917, in which the British expressed support of a Jewish "national home" in Palestine. But the declaration also stated, "It [is] clearly understood that nothing shall be done which may prejudice

A Gift from God?

Jewish fundamentalists point to Genesis 15:18, a passage in the Bible, as proof that Israelis were given their land by God. Genesis 15:18 tells of a promise made by God to Abraham in which God said, "To your descendants I give this land, from the river Wadi-el-Arish of Egypt to the great river, the Euphrates."[1] These boundaries today would include Syria, Lebanon, Kuwait, Jordan, part of Egypt, the north portion of Saudi Arabia, and approximately half of Iraq.

the civil and religious rights of existing non-Jewish communities in Palestine."[2] It did not, however, mention political rights.

The Jewish people felt that Israel was their home, their promised land, where they should be safe. The creation of the state of Israel in 1948 was the culmination of a dream the Zionists held for generations. They refused to give it up, even in the face of hostilities that continue to this day.

Terrorist Attacks on Both Sides

In the long Arab-Israeli conflict, people on both sides have committed atrocities. Arabs still commemorate the Deir Yassin massacre on April 9, 1948. During that event, Jewish forces attacked an Arab village and executed approximately 120 people, many of them women and children.

Israelis have regularly suffered bombings, shellings, shootings, and rocket attacks, most of which targeted civilians. In 1951, Arabs killed or injured more than 150 Israelis. The Munich Olympics murders were links in a chain of attacks and retaliations that continue today.

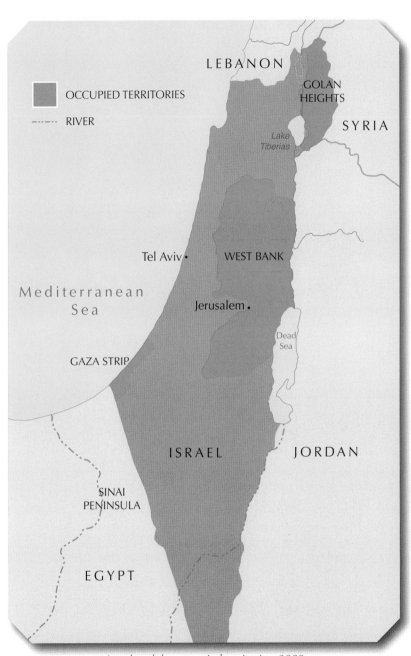

Israel and the occupied territories, 2009

Yasser Arafat became chairman of the Palestine Liberation Organization and helped create the terrorist group Black September.

BEFORE MUNICH

n May 1967, armies from Syria, Jordan, and Egypt began assembling on the borders of Israel. Fearing an attack, Israel decided to strike first. Israel launched an attack on Egypt, destroying its grounded air force and then pushing into the Sinai Peninsula in Egypt. Jordan soon began attacking Israel, and Israel responded by taking control of the Old City of Jerusalem and the West Bank from Jordan. On the fifth day of fighting, Syria attacked, and Israel took the Golan Heights from Syria one day later. The war lasted only six days before the United Nations stepped in and arranged a cease-fire. In the end, Israel had overpowered its neighbors and gained control over the disputed Sinai Peninsula, Gaza Strip, West Bank, Golan Heights, and the Old City of Jerusalem. This would only increase tension between the two sides.

In the aftermath of the 1967 Six-Day War, several militant groups took control of the Palestine Liberation Organization (PLO), a political group representing the Palestinian people. Its goal was to create an independent Palestinian state, replacing Israel. The largest militant group was Fatah, which had been attacking Israel since 1965.

Fatah

Fatah is a political and military group founded by Yasser Arafat in the late 1950s that opposed Israeli control of Palestinian territory. The organization used terrorist-style raids against Israel and did not recognize Israel's right to exist.

By 1970, Fatah had taken control of the PLO and later created the terrorist group Black September. In 1988, Fatah recognized Israel's right to exist and now supports a two-state solution for an independent Palestinian state on the West Bank and the Gaza Strip. Fatah runs the Palestinian Authority, which governs Palestinian-held West Bank, and seeks legitimate statehood.

The leader of Fatah, Yasser Arafat, was elected chairman of the PLO in 1969.

THE BIRTH OF BLACK SEPTEMBER

The PLO did not recognize Israel's right to exist and often launched attacks on Israel. But Arafat and his PLO lieutenants knew that an association with terrorism could give the PLO a negative image globally. And it would hamper the goal of establishing a Palestinian state. The result was the terrorist group Black September, named in honor of the Palestinians killed when Jordan forced the PLO out of the country in September 1970.

Black September

In the 1960s, the Jordanian monarchy hosted PLO guerrilla camps. These camps were made up of heavily armed Fatah soldiers, called *fedayeen,* who staged raids in Israel. Jordan's King Hussein supported the raids on Israel. But he became concerned when the Palestinians began to flex their muscle inside his kingdom. Over time, Fatah forces gained enough power in Jordan to begin claiming control of some of its territory.

In September 1970, King Hussein declared martial law. The Jordanian army attacked the fedayeen, who enlisted support from Syrian forces. The Jordanian air force attacked Syrian tanks. Fatah tried to enlist additional aid from Iraq and Egypt. Both declined, fearing a Middle East war.

The Jordanian army defeated the fedayeen, killing approximately 4,000 soldiers and driving the rest into Lebanon. Palestinians saw the event as a betrayal of Arabs by fellow Arabs and called it Black September. The Black September terrorist group was named in commemoration of the deaths of the 4,000 Palestinian fedayeen in Jordan.

Black September skimmed the best personnel from Fatah's militia. The group's organizers were young university-educated men and women from Fatah's intelligence department. The best of Fatah's elite fighters joined the "special services division" that carried out terrorist attacks. The funding and direction of Black September were kept separate from Fatah so that it could deny responsibility for Black September's acts.

The Munich attack was not Black September's first. In 1972, the group began killing Arabs who collaborated with Israel and attacking businesses with Israeli interests. In May 1972, the group attempted to hijack a plane bound for Tel Aviv, Israel, but the mission ended in failure. Israeli troops stormed the plane, killing or capturing all the terrorists. Since then, morale among Palestinian militants had been low. The Munich attack was meant to change that.

BLACK SEPTEMBER LEADERSHIP

Black September had two levels. The inner circle planned and carried out attacks. A less informed outer circle provided support. People in the outer circle were told only what they needed to know in order to do their jobs. Volunteers might carry a suitcase, never asking what was inside, or buy plane tickets for people they did not know.

Salah Khalaf, known as Abu Iyad, was Black September's leader. He was one of Arafat's main deputies and a commander in the Fatah militia. One of Abu Iyad's followers, Mohammed Oudeh, known as Abu Daoud, was the mastermind of the Munich attack. Another of Abu Iyad's trusted lieutenants was Fakhri Al-Omri, a brilliant strategist. None of these men involved themselves in the attack itself, but they were instrumental in choosing the team and planning the assault.

Covert Cell Systems

Militias often organize themselves based on a cell system designed to resist infiltration. Black September was no exception. Members of one cell are acquainted only with the people in their own cell but not with those in other cells. If an agent turns against former comrades, he can betray only a few people. A cell receives supplies, information, and orders from a single person who manages the agents in only one or two cells. Even the highest-ranking members of the organization might not be aware of all the cells.

THE TERRORISTS

The Munich terrorist team was chosen from a group of elite fighters from a Fatah training camp south of Beirut, Lebanon. There, 50 men competed for the opportunity to be chosen for a mission they knew nothing about. They fired AK-47 assault rifles and practiced lobbing the F-1 hand grenades that would be used with deadly effect in

The Fatah Hawks, a militant wing of the PLO,
marched through the Gaza Strip in 1994.

Munich. The 27-year-old leader of the terrorists,
Muhammad Massalha, called himself Issa. He
had a personal motive for the attack. Issa hoped
to exchange hostages for the freedom of his two
brothers, fellow Black September militants who were
in Israeli jails.

Yussef Nazzal, or Tony, was second in command.
According to Abu Iyad, Tony was the brains behind
the mission. He was 25 years old and spoke fluent
German. Tony visited Munich months before the

attack to analyze the layout of the Olympic Village and look for potential points of entry.

The other terrorists included Mohammed Safady, Jamal Al-Gashey, and Jamal's uncle Adnan Al-Gashey. Three others, Khalid Jawad, Ahmed Sheik, and Afif Ahmed Hamid, were likely chosen because they had lived in Germany.

Preparations for the Assault

Once chosen, the team was transported to Libya for intensive training. This involved sprints, leaping, and scaling walls and fences. They were told nothing of their mission; they had no idea that they were being prepared to scale the wall around the Olympic Village in Munich. The grueling training, much of it in extreme heat, gave the terrorists the lean, muscular builds that later helped them pass as Olympians.

A Missed Opportunity

Shmuel Lalkin was the head of the Israeli Olympic delegation. He discovered that security was lax before the Games even began. Lalkin toured all the facilities on a pre-Olympic visit to Munich, including the apartments that were later targeted. At the time, he relayed his concerns to the Munich police department. He did not like that the apartments were on the first floor and so close to the perimeter of the Olympic Village. He wanted his athletes moved. The German officials promised security would be tight but refused to move the athletes. When Lalkin tried to contact Israeli security officials, he was ignored. He had little influence since security was not part of his job.

A Dismissive Response

Shmuel Lalkin wrote a letter to Arie Shumar, chief security officer of the Education, Culture, and Sports Ministry. He outlined his concerns about security for the Israeli athletes. He received the following response:
"Dear Mr. Lalkin:
As Manager of the Israeli Olympic team it would be advisable for you to concentrate on sports. Leave security to the security personnel.
Yours Truly,
Arie Shumar."[1]

The Israeli Delegation

When the Israeli delegation arrived in Munich in the summer of 1972, it had more athletes, coaches, and officials than any previous Israeli Olympic delegation. Still, many Israelis were wary about being in Germany. It turned out their concerns were valid—but not because that European country posed a threat. Within days, 11 Israelis were taken hostage and later killed at the hands of Palestinian terrorists.

The 11 captured Israelis were athletes, coaches, and referees who, like many Israelis, came from a variety of backgrounds. The first man killed, Moshe Weinberg, was an Israeli-born wrestling coach. Two of the wrestlers he coached, Eliezer Halfin and Mark Slavin, were born in the former Soviet Union and also taken hostage. Weight lifter Yossef Romano, the second hostage killed, was born in Libya.

The other hostages included weight lifter David Berger (born in the United States), weight lifter Ze'ev Friedman (Siberia), wrestling referee Yossef Gutfreund, head track coach Amitzur Shapira (Israel), marksmen coach Kehat Shorr (Romania), fencing coach Andre Spitzer (Romania), and weight lifting referee Yaakov Springer (Poland). Only light-flyweight freestyle wrestler Gad Tsabari was captured and managed to escape.

The Israeli delegation had a fabulous evening before the attack. They attended a performance of *Fiddler on the Roof* and were invited backstage to meet the cast. Shmuel Lalkin brought along his wife, Yardena, and their 13-year-old son, Arik. Little did they know what would wake them just a few hours later.

*Israeli weight lifter Yossef Romano competed
at the 1972 Munich Olympics.*

The apartments at 31 Connollystrasse, where the 11 captured Israelis stayed during the Munich Olympics, shown in 2002

TAKING HOSTAGES

The terrorists could have been stopped when their weapons entered Germany. Black September used a couple of *saya'an*—outer circle volunteers—to smuggle in AK-47s and grenades in advance. They would not carry their own weapons.

Young men traveling with lots of baggage would have
been too suspicious, and the best fighters would go
to jail if the weapons were found in their baggage.
Instead, a middle-aged man and a woman posing as
his wife took the weapons. The couple had no idea
what was inside the four suitcases—only that safe
delivery would aid the Palestinian cause.

The saya'an were stopped in customs, and
officials began to search their bags. The man lost his
temper and shouted at them. It made no difference;
the officials continued anyway. They chose a bag
to open. It was full of lingerie. The woman made
a show of being annoyed by strangers handling her
intimate items. Embarrassed, the customs officials
let the couple go. They never opened the other
three bags, which contained eight submachine guns,
ammunition, and ten grenades. The couriers left the
bags in lockers at the Munich central railway station
and dropped the keys at the desk of a nearby hotel.
Their job was done. A Black September commander
picked up the weapons later.

SLOPPY SECURITY

The perimeter fence around the Olympic Village
was about six feet (1.8 m) high and topped with metal

cones instead of barbed wire. The gates were guarded during the day, but security was lax. Gates were locked at midnight, leaving late-night partiers only one way to get back to their dorms: over the fence. Security stopped worrying about athletes coming in that way.

Ignoring Their Own Expert

In preparation for the Munich Games, West German organizers hired police psychologist Doctor Georg Sieber to predict possible security threats. Sieber's job was to think like a terrorist and write scenarios of potential attacks. One of his 26 predictions was eerily accurate. In this scenario, terrorists scaled the wall around the Olympic Village at 5:00 a.m., took athletes hostage, and killed several to show that they meant business. They demanded the release of prisoners from Israeli jails and a plane to fly them to an Arab country, or the hostages would die. The terrorists were prepared to die and would kill their hostages rather than fail.

The German organizers asked Sieber for a set of less drastic scenarios. They thought drunken fans and ticket scalping were the worst they could expect. Their real problem was that, in order to prepare for a crisis, security would need to be armed and visible. Organizers feared that armed security guards would be far too reminiscent of Nazis. They could not deal with a threat while appearing open and friendly, so they did not deal with the threat at all.

Issa, the terrorist leader, knew the Olympic Village well. He and Tony had taken jobs there to learn the layout. Shortly after 4:00 a.m. on September 5, 1972, Issa took his team to gate 25A. He knew that was the easiest place to cross. The terrorists were dressed in red tracksuits and carried duffel bags decorated with the Olympic rings. They looked like Olympians. However, there was a deadly arsenal inside each bag. In a later interview, surviving terrorist Jamal Al-Gashey recalled the tension he felt as his team approached the fence. They met a U.S. team coming back from a night out. The Americans mistook them for fellow athletes. "We got to chatting," Jamal later said, "and then we helped each other over."[1]

Tony had scouted out the building a few days earlier. The terrorists already knew exactly where the Israelis were sleeping. The street door to the building was unlocked. The team walked right into the shared foyer outside apartment one. From the foyer, a flight of stairs led down to the parking garage, and another flight led to the upper-level apartments.

The terrorists had used an inside connection to obtain a key to apartment one. It must have been a bad copy. The sounds of the key persistently jiggling in the lock woke Yossef Gutfreund, a 40-year-old referee. Gutfreund got out of bed and walked to

Blending In

There was no tactical reason for the terrorists to change out of their tracksuits. But before the attack, just outside the Israelis' building, they all took the time to change their clothes. This hints that these young men were acutely aware of the media attention that would surround them. Issa, their spokesman, wore a tan safari suit and a dapper white hat, but his face was blackened with shoe polish.

the door to see who was there. The door opened a few inches, and he saw terrorists holding assault rifles. He shouted and tried to slam the door shut. The Palestinians threw their shoulders against the door, pushing against him.

Weight lifting trainer Tuvia Sokolovsky heard the noise and came over to see what was going on. "Through the half-open door, I saw a man with a black-painted face holding a weapon. At that moment I knew I had to escape."[2] He started screaming to wake the others and ran to his window. He desperately pounded on it, but the window would not open.

Gutfreund was a powerful man—approximately 6 feet 4 inches (193 cm) tall and 290 pounds (131.5 kg)—but he was outnumbered. He held the door against the terrorists for as long as he could. The terrorists used the butts of their Kalishnikov rifles to wedge the door open and braced their feet on the wall behind them. Gutfreund held on with all his power, but it was not enough. The terrorists burst in, forcing him to the floor at gunpoint.

Just then, Sokolovsky's window broke open. He leaped out and took off. In bare feet and wearing only his pajamas, he ran for his life. A terrorist fired on him as he ran. Sokolovsky heard bullets whistling past him. He ran to the shelter of a raised concrete flowerbed and hid there. Next door in apartment two, race walker Shaul Ladany heard the sound of gunfire and escaped.

Inside apartment one, terrorists rounded up the Israelis. Coaches Amitzur Shapira and Kehat Shorr were dragged out of bed at gunpoint. Wrestling coach Moshe Weinberg refused to go quietly. He armed himself with all he had—a fruit knife. Weinberg slashed at Issa when he had the chance, but he managed only to cut Issa's jacket. Issa's backup man shot Weinberg but did not kill him.

The bullet entered the side of Weinberg's mouth and went out the other side of his cheek, missing his brain. Tony and several other terrorists dragged him down the hall

A Holocaust Survivor Escapes Again

Tuvia Sokolovsky, the man who escaped through the window, never felt safe in Germany. "I am a Holocaust survivor. For me, Germans and Munich mean the extermination of 6 million Jews, including my father and his family. I had a horrible feeling as I saw in every adult German the face of the murderers of my parents."[4]

toward the other apartments. The terrorists aimed to capture all of the Israelis that they could. Weinberg's damaged face sent the message that they were serious.

In apartment one, Issa and the remaining two Fatah soldiers tied up fencing coach Andre Spitzer, weight lifting referee Yaakov Springer, and Gutfreund, who had tried to hold the door closed.

No one knows what Weinberg said to the terrorists that caused them to pass by apartment two. Weinberg knew that the light, quick fencers were in apartment two along with the marksmen and the race walker Ladany. His plan might have been to take the terrorists to the wrestlers and weight lifters in apartment three. These men had a better chance of overpowering the terrorists.

The first to be caught in apartment three were the two Russian-born wrestlers, Mark Slavin, who came to Israel to escape anti-Semitism, and the mechanic Eliezer Halfin. By now, the terrorists had abandoned any pretense of stealth. The noise awoke flyweight wrestler Gad Tsabari. He opened his door to see his teammates held at gunpoint. Tsabari was caught. Moments later, so were American-born weight lifter David Berger and his teammate Ze'ev Friedman from Siberia.

*Blood stained the floor of the room where the terrorists
kept the Israeli hostages.*

The terrorists decided to hold their hostages
in the upstairs bedroom of apartment one. To get
there, they had to go outside the building and back
in through the foyer entrance. They lined up the
hostages and marched them military-prisoner style
with hands on their heads. As they marched, Berger
exclaimed in Hebrew, "Let's pounce on them! We
have nothing to lose!"[5] Unfortunately, one of the
terrorists understood him and prodded him along
with his rifle.

As they passed the stairs into the underground parking garage, Tsabari saw his chance. With the quickness that flyweight wrestlers are known for, the 106-pound (48 kg) man broke out of line and ran down the stairs. A terrorist pursued him, firing as he ran. "I felt two or three rounds being shot at me. I ran for my life, zigzagging to avoid the salvo of shots. I could not believe that none of them hit me," Tsabari later said.[6]

The injured Weinberg took advantage of the distraction and attacked 19-year-old terrorist Mohammed Safady. He punched Safady so hard he fractured the teenager's jaw and knocked out a couple of his teeth. Then he grabbed for Safady's gun. Another terrorist shot Weinberg in the chest before he could use the gun.

This time, the shot killed Moshe Weinberg. The terrorists marched their hostages into apartment one, leaving Weinberg's body behind on the floor.

A police officer blocking the entrance of Munich's Olympic Village

A police officer looked at the apartments where the Black September terrorists held 11 Israeli hostages.

BROKEN PROMISES, SHATTERED LIVES

The terrorists brought their hostages from apartment three to the bedroom where Amitzur Shapira, Kehat Shorr, Andre Spitzer, Yaakov Springer, and Yossef Gutfreund were already tied up. As Yossef Romano entered the bedroom with his captors, he must have seen that the other men were tied and that he would soon join them.

Romano was a large man whose wild, curly black hair made him look even larger than he was. The weight lifter was on crutches after being injured in competition. Even in this condition, the former military man was capable of lifting more than 400 pounds (181 kg). He picked that moment to attack. Romano charged a terrorist and grabbed for his gun. He got the gun, but he never had a chance to use it. Another militant shot him a number of times at close range. Romano was dead.

The terrorists tied up David Berger, Ze'ev Friedman, Eliezer Halfin, and Mark Slavin with the others. Romano's body remained where he fell.

WORD GOT OUT

It is possible that the press heard the news of the hostage crisis before the authorities. Tsabari, the wrestler who escaped through the parking

Ilana's Premonition

Ilana Romano had a bad feeling about the Munich Olympics in which her husband Yossef would compete. As the Games neared, her fears worsened. She talked to Yossef about it, but he had no worries. He trusted the Germans to organize everything perfectly. On September 5, Ilana heard that Yossef was one of the hostages. She feared the worst, knowing it was in his nature to put up a fight. She was right. Yossef was the second hostage to die.

garage, jumped over the perimeter fence and went straight to the press center outside. He was barefoot and wearing little clothing, so some Germans loaned him sandals and oversized clothes. Tsabari told his story to journalists before he was taken to meet with Olympic officials.

The terrorists saw race walker Ladany as he slipped out of apartment two. Jamal Al-Gashey later explained that he thought everyone from that apartment had fled. Actually, athlete Henry Herskowitz, who had carried the Israeli flag in the opening ceremony, and his roommates were still hiding inside. Ladany woke some Americans, who helped him call the police. Herskowitz and his roommates escaped later.

THE LONG STANDOFF BEGINS

Munich Chief of Police Manfred Schreiber was called in. Word spread throughout the German government and to Prime Minister Golda Meir in Israel. Police cordoned off the area around the apartment where the hostages were being held. However, the day went on as usual elsewhere in the Olympic Village. An equestrian dressage competition was scheduled to begin at 8:00 a.m.

Schreiber sent an officer to Connollystrasse a little after 5:00 a.m. to see what was going on. A terrorist saw the officer coming and threw several sheets of paper out the window. The officer, aware of the AK-47s at the window above him, grabbed the papers and left. The typewritten sheets listed Black September's demands: the release of 234 prisoners in Israel, as well as two in German prisons: Ulrike Meinhof and Andreas Baader, members of the German Baader-Meinhof terrorist gang that was known to work with Palestinian terrorists. Among the prisoners in Israeli jails were Issa's two militant brothers.

The deadline was 9:00 a.m., or the hostages would be executed. To prove they meant it, the terrorists dumped Weinberg's body in the street outside. Lalkin and Herskowitz watched in horror from their windows in apartment two.

Schreiber, Olympic Village Mayor Walther Tröger, and other German officials gathered in anxious

The Baader-Meinhof Gang

The Baader-Meinhof Gang was a German terrorist group that attacked targets in their own country, mostly between 1968 and 1977. They were disillusioned with capitalist society and wanted to trigger a world revolution ending in communism. The gang robbed banks and firebombed stores, killing many civilians. The gang was unusual in that it had a relatively large proportion of young female members, including leader Andreas Baader's girlfriend, Gudrun Ensslin, who, despite the name of the gang, was actually second in command, above Ulrike Meinhof.

Manfred Schreiber, Munich's chief of police, center, *discussed the deadline with Issa,* right.

meetings. Police officer Anneliese Graes volunteered to meet with Issa. Graes tried to tell Issa that the Germans had no control over prisoners in Israel. Issa still insisted that they release the prisoners or else all of the hostages would be killed.

Television coverage of the Olympic Games was interspersed with scenes of the terrorists. Issa was seen on the balcony in his linen safari suit, his face partially obscured by black shoe polish, sunglasses, and a white hat pulled down over his eyes. As a silent warning, he always held either a grenade or an AK-47. Second-in-command Tony looked out the second floor window, a gold chain gleaming from under his unbuttoned shirt. The press nicknamed him "the Cowboy" for his wide-brimmed gray hat, red shirt, and the revolver on his hip.

The Deadline Approaches

Perhaps Issa knew that his 9:00 a.m. deadline was impossible. Or perhaps that poor choice was due only to his youth and inexperience. Even if the governments of Israel and Germany had wanted to release the prisoners—which they had no intention of doing—they could never have found and released them all so quickly. Negotiators did not tell Issa that. Their idea was to string him along, promising endlessly that his demands were being met while trying to come up with a plan.

As the deadline approached, Issa agreed to meet with a delegation of German and Olympic officials. Chief Schreiber, Mayor Tröger, and A. D. Touney, an Egyptian member of the International Olympic Committee (IOC), spoke with Issa outside the apartment. The terrorists' automatic weapons were trained on them from above the entire time.

The much larger men dwarfed Issa. But Issa clutched his hand grenade, ready to use it if any moves were made against him. Despite the tension, Issa appeared to believe Touney when he promised that prisoner releases were under way. Issa readily agreed to extend the deadline to noon.

ISRAEL REFUSES TO GIVE IN

At 11:15 that morning, the German police learned that the Israeli government was not going to release any prisoners. Israelis had a policy of never complying with terrorists' demands because that encouraged future attacks. The Israelis were fully aware that this decision might cost the athletes their lives, but more was at stake. Golda Meir explained, "If we should give in, then no Israeli anywhere in the world will feel that his life is safe. It's blackmail of the worst kind."[1]

No Turning Back

Olympic Village Mayor Walther Tröger established a rapport with Issa. He and Issa spent part of the day discussing politics. At one point, Tröger turned to Issa and said, "Listen, why don't you give up?" Issa said, "We are dead anyway, either we will be killed here, or if we go out and give up without having hostages . . . we will be killed where we go."[3]

German officials had no idea what to do, and discipline was breaking down. A Stasi (German secret police) file later noted that the police appeared "more hysterical than in control."[2]

THREE BRAVE GERMANS

Issa extended his deadline again, to 1:00 p.m., but he was losing patience. This time, he swore that two hostages would be executed on television if his terms were not met. High-ranking negotiators were brought in. These included Hans-Dietrich Genscher, the

The Unit Prepares for Action

The *Sayeret Matkal*, also known as "the Unit," was a secret elite Israeli army force. The Unit was specially trained in antiterrorist tactics and hostage rescue. If any group had the capabilities to rescue the hostages, it was the Unit. Like the members of some elite fighting forces today, its men were trained to withstand torture, so they were better equipped to keep secrets.

Muki Betser, the platoon commander, was not sure if the Unit would be deployed. He thought the Germans might have an elite antiterrorist squad of their own. They did not—the Germans did not even have a special weapons and tactics (SWAT) team. The regular police department was handling the hostage crisis. Because the Unit was a military force, it could not enter Germany without permission from the government. Without clearance, the group's weapons and equipment would surely be stopped at the border.

The Unit was put on alert. The men were dressed in civilian clothes and their equipment was packed. They sat ready for hours, but the call to take off never came. The Germans refused to give the Israelis permission to send in their team. They chose to deal with the situation themselves.

German interior minister; Bruno
Merck, the Bavarian interior
minister; and Hans-Jochen Vogel,
mayor of Munich. They continued
to tell Issa that prisoners were in
the process of being released. Issa
apparently believed them. However,
the delays could not go on forever.
Genscher, Tröger, and Vogel offered
to switch places with the hostages. Issa
repeatedly refused.

Issa became more and more
agitated as time went on. Soon,
4:00 p.m. passed, and then
5:00 p.m. He realized that he
was being manipulated. Issa did not
want to kill the hostages. Dead men
were of no use in an exchange. He
had few options, and the pressure
was mounting.

Games Suspended

Some athletes and spectators wanted the Games to go on, regardless of the hostage crisis. Golda Meir thought otherwise, and many others agreed with her. They felt that it was obscene to play games when lives were at stake. The International Olympic Committee finally caved to pressure and suspended the Games for the afternoon on September 5. A memorial for the dead athletes was scheduled for the next day.

Issa, in white hat, spoke with another terrorist while negotiating with German and Olympics officials.

A West German helicopter prepared to land in the Olympic Village
and pick up the terrorists and their hostages.

THE BITTER END

By early evening of September 5,
1972, terrorists and negotiators were
exhausted. The terrorists had been awake for more
than 24 hours. Everyone's patience was wearing
thin. Issa remained committed to his cause. He even

rejected a $9 million payoff. At one point he said, "Talk of money is demeaning."[1]

Instead, Issa offered another alternative: the Germans could arrange a flight for his team and their hostages to an Arab country where negotiations would continue. Many Germans saw this as a blow to their pride. They wanted to show the world that Germans could handle the situation themselves with no help from Israel or the international community.

Hans-Dietrich Genscher, the German interior minister, wanted to know if the hostages were opposed to being flown to an Arab country. He did not trust Issa; he needed to ask them personally. The terrorists allowed Genscher and Olympic Village Mayor Tröger to enter the upstairs bedroom of apartment one. What they saw was appalling. The floor was littered with garbage, pooled blood, and human waste. Walls were marked with bullet holes and blood. Yossef Romano's body was on the floor. Hostages sat four to a bed, bound hand and foot. Genscher and Tröger counted four or five terrorists. There were actually eight. This mistake came back later to haunt them.

Hopeful for a resolution, the hostages agreed to fly to Egypt. The Germans never intended to let this happen. They only made the promise to get the hostages out of the well-guarded apartment so they could attempt a rescue.

LEGENDARY INCOMPETENCE

The Germans made several plans to save the hostages. The first was a feeble attempt to jump the terrorists as they picked up food that Issa requested. The food was delivered in four separate containers in the hopes that four militants would come out to carry the boxes. Police dressed as chefs then planned to ambush the terrorists. They were disappointed when Issa carried the crates indoors by himself, one at a time.

Perhaps the most criticized of the German plans was "Operation Sunshine." The Munich terrorist attack was the first in history to be televised live, and a crowd of approximately 80,000 people had gathered outside the Olympic Village. Though the police cordoned off the immediate area, news crews were filming from windows of buildings across the street.

As part of Operation Sunshine, two German policemen approached the apartment where the Israeli hostages were being held.

The police sent a team of martial arts experts onto the roof of the apartment building. In a futile attempt to blend with athletes, the officers wore tracksuits over their sidearms and bulletproof vests. Some openly carried machine guns. The plan called for police to drop in through air conditioning vents and windows. They would surprise the terrorists and disarm them of their assault rifles, handguns, and grenades. But the television crews filmed every move and broadcast live footage while commentators counted down to the moment of the strike. People all over the world watched the police crawl up onto the roof and take their positions. The terrorists also watched on the television in apartment one. Furious, Issa ran outside, threatening to kill hostages unless the men got off the roof. The police sheepishly retreated. In a later interview, one of the officers said, "Thank God they called it off. It would have been a suicide mission."[2]

A Series of Fatal Errors

While Israel's elite counterterrorist force was forbidden to enter Germany, ordinary police officers carried out the hostage rescue under the command of Georg Wolf, deputy to the police chief. The plan was to transport terrorists and their hostages by helicopter to Fürstenfeldbruck military airfield.

A Lufthansa Boeing 727 sat on the runway, apparently ready to fly to Egypt. But the Germans never

No Knockout Gas

In the initial stages of the hostage crisis, the German police heard a rumor that the police department in Chicago, Illinois, had developed a nonlethal knockout gas. This sounded like a perfect solution—the hostages could be rescued and the terrorists would wake up in prison. Unfortunately, when the German police contacted the Chicago police, they learned that there was no such gas in production at that time.

intended for it to take off, and it would not even
have a real pilot aboard. Police would wear Lufthansa
uniforms and pose as the captain and crew. When
Issa and Tony came to inspect the aircraft, the
disguised officers would shoot them. Once Issa and
Tony were down, sharpshooters were to pick off the
other terrorists. Armored vehicles would then swoop
in and rescue the hostages. The plan seemed simple
enough, but almost everything went wrong.

Initially, police set up an ambush in the
underground parking garage. Hidden gunmen
were ready to kill the terrorists as they moved to the
helicopter. Issa checked out the route beforehand
and spotted a few clumsy snipers crawling away. He
demanded that a bus take them to the helicopters.
That plan was ruined.

As the eight terrorists loaded their prisoners
onto the helicopter, Bavarian Prime Minister Franz
Joseph Strauss exclaimed, "Hey, they got the number
of terrorists wrong!"[3] Journalist Peter Jennings also
reported this fact on television, but no one thought
to notify the police at the airport. Thinking they had
four or five terrorists instead of eight, the police had
only five snipers. This was another fatal error.

The next in this series of disasters was the mutiny of a crucial police team. The officers scheduled to pose as crew on the airliner decided theirs was a suicide mission and backed out. After the team had accepted the mission, they realized that the plane held a full tank of fuel that would ignite if touched off by a bullet or an exploding grenade. The entire plane would go up in flames with them in it. And yet, the tank could have been drained earlier if anyone had taken the initiative.

The team members also thought their disguises were terrible. Lufthansa uniforms could not be found to fit everyone. Some were wearing Lufthansa

Erroneous Reports of Rescue

A rumor that all the hostages had been rescued started in the crowd outside the gates of Fürstenfeldbruck military airfield. It spread and was eventually picked up by news agencies that presented it as fact. Even Conrad Ahlers, the German chancellor's press secretary, went on television to spread the good news. Celebrations broke out across the Olympic Village and in athletes' homes, where neighbors brought over flowers and champagne. In Israel, Golda Meir watched the television reports and breathed a sigh of relief.

Several of the athletes' wives hesitated to celebrate until they knew for sure that their husbands were safe. Ankie Spitzer was the wife of fencing coach Andre Spitzer and the mother of his infant daughter. She told her supporters, "Andre will call and when we hear his voice, we'll celebrate."[4]

Everyone waited, but the hoped-for calls never came. The truth came out after 3:00 a.m. the following morning.

jackets over their police uniform pants. In an unprecedented move, their commanding officer held a vote. Did they want to risk their lives to save the Israeli athletes? The answer was unanimous. They deserted the aircraft moments before the helicopters carrying the terrorists and their hostages arrived at the airport.

TRAGIC AND UNNECESSARY DEATHS

It was already dark outside when the terrorists landed at the airport. Lights shone from towers surrounding the aircraft. Issa and Tony left two men outside the helicopters while they checked the aircraft. They were infuriated to find it deserted. As they headed back to the helicopter, the snipers began shooting. They missed Issa, who ran for cover while shooting short, controlled bursts at the building and control tower. The snipers shot Tony in the foot, which put him out of the fight. One terrorist took cover and returned fire; another was killed.

Lack of Marksmanship

In 1972, police in Germany did not rely on firearms the way U.S. police did. When trying to find snipers for the hostage rescue effort, ranking officers were said to have asked around for anyone who had ever fired a gun. Several snipers were selected because of their participation in a shooting competition. One sniper from the airfield later admitted that he was unqualified. He had no special training in marksmanship and fired a pistol only occasionally as a hobby. Additionally, the guns provided to the snipers were not the highly accurate weapons generally used by SWAT forces. This explains why snipers missed their targets so frequently during the shootout at the airfield.

A police officer standing in front of the wreckage from the helicopter that was destroyed by a grenade

The militants quickly took out all the lights with grenades and gunfire. The Germans had not anticipated this. Now they could not identify people in the dark. One sniper was shot and wounded when his own team thought he was a terrorist. A German police officer who was watching from a window died when a bullet hit his head. Jamal Al-Gashey took a bullet in the finger, which also mangled his gun. In the darkness, everyone became confused and could not tell friends from enemies.

The hostages were still trapped in the helicopters. Israeli envoys pleaded for police to rescue the prisoners. The commander refused to risk his officers' lives and insisted on waiting for armored vehicles to perform the attack. The vehicles should have been sent over ahead of time, but the Germans had forgotten about that detail. The vehicles had finally been ordered to the airfield nearly 20 minutes into the confrontation.

Those vehicles were delayed, however. Earlier, when helicopters soared over the crowd outside 31 Connollystrasse, swarms of people jumped into their cars and followed. The armored vehicles got caught in traffic and were hours late.

When the armored vehicles rolled onto the darkened tarmac, the terrorists knew they did not have a chance. These vehicles could follow them and fire on them wherever they hid. The fanatical young militants wanted to strike a blow against Israel that would not be forgotten. They would not be killed or captured while allowing their prisoners to escape. A terrorist tossed a grenade into one helicopter. Another terrorist gunned down the hostages inside the other helicopter. Then, they ran into the darkness.

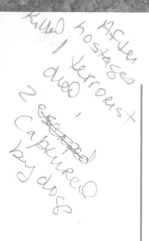

A sniper picked off Issa, who fell dead before making it off the tarmac. Jamal and Adnan Al-Gashey ran into the surrounding fields along with Mohammed Safady. They stayed ahead of their pursuers for more than an hour, but they could not hide from packs of German shepherd tracking dogs. They were captured and jailed.

The German Excuse

The day after the tragedy, Chief Schreiber told the press, "Some people say that police mistakes caused the deaths of the hostages. But it was the other way around. The hostages died because the terrorists made no mistakes."[5] The Germans would not take responsibility for their failures for many years. They would finally relent only because of unceasing pressure from the victims' families.

The Autopsy

David Berger received two nonlethal gunshot wounds during the firefight at the airfield. If the German police had pulled him from the burning helicopter, he would have survived. An autopsy showed that he died of smoke inhalation.

Flags flew at half-staff around the Olympic torch on September 6, 1972.

Members of the Israeli delegation put black ribbons in their front pockets to honor their murdered comrades.

VENGEANCE

On October 29, 1972, Black September hijacked a Lufthansa Boeing 727 on its way from Beirut, Lebanon, to Frankfurt, Germany. The hijackers demanded to land in Munich and pick up the three surviving terrorists from the Olympic

massacre. The German government agreed and
sent the three Palestinians to Riem airport. Possibly
fearing a double-cross, the hijackers diverted their
plane to Zagreb, Yugoslavia, and insisted that the
terrorists who had been taken prisoner be brought
there instead. They forced the plane to circle above
Zagreb until it was seconds from running out of fuel.
The hijackers allowed the pilot to land just in time to
avoid killing everyone on board.

Meanwhile, the prisoners were on their way to
Yugoslavia by helicopter. When they arrived, they
triumphantly boarded the hijacked plane. However,
the hostages aboard the flight were not freed as
promised. They were forced to accompany the
terrorists to Libya, where they were released.

German officials and historians agree that the
hijacking was probably prearranged between the
German government and the PLO. The presence of
the imprisoned terrorists in their country worried
the Germans, who feared becoming the target of new
attacks. A staged hijacking was a way for the Germans
to release the terrorists without looking bad before
the international community.

The circumstances of the hijacking are suspicious.
The aircraft left Damascus, Syria, with no passengers

at all. Profit-minded airlines do not normally choose to move aircraft around without defraying the cost with paying passengers. Only 13 passengers boarded in Beirut, including the two hijackers, and none of them were women or children. Curiously, the German government obeyed the hijackers instantly, with no attempt at negotiation or resistance.

A Heroes' Welcome

The arrival of the three terrorists in Libya set off celebrations all across the Middle East. The three men held a news conference in Tripoli, Libya, where they proudly acknowledged their part in the Munich operation. In Arab nations, they were hailed as heroes who successfully made the plight of the Palestinian people known to the world.

A Secret Squad of Assassins

The Germans released the three terrorists without informing Israel. When Israeli Prime Minister Golda

Meir heard the killers were free, she ordered Mossad, Israel's Central Institute for Intelligence and Security, to hunt them down. Any saya'ans, or helpers, who had aided the terrorists were targeted, too. This order did not expire with the end of Golda Meir's term. Conspirators were still not safe as many as 20 years after the Munich Olympics.

By the 1970s, Mossad had developed into a superior counterterrorist unit. Its special operations unit gathered information about upcoming attacks on Israelis at home and in other countries. Professional assassins roved throughout the Middle East and Europe, tracking down and killing terrorists and the saya'ans who supported them. The organization gained a reputation for being able to strike with devastating effect anywhere, at any time.

Accusations of Anti-Semitism

The inability of German officials to handle even the smallest detail of the hostage crisis has led some historians to wonder if anti-Semitism was at the root of the failure. No one will ever know their motives for sure, and personal feelings must have varied among individuals. Certainly, German Interior Minister Hans-Dietrich Genscher, Munich Mayor Hans-Jochen Vogel, and Olympic Village Mayor Walther Tröger will be remembered for their brave offer to switch places with the hostages. They would have died to save the athletes, but certain police officers refused to even carry out their duties.

REVENGE

Mossad Assassins

Many of the terrorist attacks against Israel targeted innocent by-standers. The Mossad assassins had a different approach. They made every attempt to kill only targeted individuals without harming their families or innocent bystanders. Surveillance went on for weeks before the attacks, and Mossad planned the killings for times when families were away.

Jews all over the world were devastated by the murders in Germany, especially since they occurred so soon after the Holocaust. During the Holocaust, nearly all of the Jews who were killed were law-abiding people. Most went along quietly when the Nazis rounded them up. Few German Jews realized that the ghettos to which the Germans were transporting them were, in fact, death camps.

That obedient mind-set changed after the Holocaust. Israelis would no longer endure persecution without retaliation. The killers had not been brought to justice, and Germany had not yet offered meaningful compensation to the 25 dependents of the slain athletes. Since the justice system had failed them, Jews were ready to take matters into their own hands.

The idea of revenge for the Munich assassinations did not play well in the court of world opinion, but it certainly motivated individual Mossad agents. In the years that followed the death of fencing coach Andre Spitzer, his widow Ankie occasionally received phone calls from unidentified men telling her to watch the news. Another terrorist had just been killed. Ankie Spitzer never asked for revenge, but one mysterious caller told her, "This is for Andre."[I]

Of course, not everyone agreed that assassination reduced terrorism. Some said that violence fed into a cycle of attacks and retaliations. This trapped the participants into perpetual war, especially in Middle Eastern

Prevention, Deterrence, and Revenge

Mossad operated under the premise that assassination fights terrorism by prevention, deterrence, and revenge. Agents tried to prevent terror attacks by striking key militants before their operations began. According to their philosophy, killing a terrorist had further-reaching effects than just preventing future attacks by that individual. If the assassin neutralized a key individual, a whole terrorist cell might collapse. Militant groups are often held together by the charisma of their leaders. Without their leader, members lose focus or disband entirely.

Mossad leaders had many reasons to believe that assassination also deterred future attacks. When numerous terrorists are tracked down and killed, potential recruits might decide that joining a certain militia is not such a good idea. Assassination also leaves terrorists looking over their shoulders in fear. They spend more time seeing to their own safety than plotting new attacks. Mossad preferred to kill terrorists rather than jailing them because extremists might still be able to orchestrate new attacks while in prison. Mossad did not want to take any chances.

The third strategy, revenge, was rarely spoken of openly, especially by government officials. Talk of protection of their citizens and bringing offenders to justice was more socially acceptable among Israeli leaders.

cultures that tend to remember offenses to ancestors. Over the years, Israeli policy regarding assassinating terrorists shifted depending on the current prime minister's philosophy.

OPERATION WRATH OF GOD

Jamal Al-Gashey, Adnan Al-Gashey, and Mohammed Safady were the three surviving terrorists from the Munich Olympics. They topped the Mossad's list of targets. Abu Iyad, the head of Black September, and his right-hand man, Abu Daoud, made the Most Wanted list, too. They had planned the Munich attack and chosen the team to carry it out.

Two of Abu Iyad's operations officers were also targeted. They were the tactical genius Fakhri Al-Omri and Atef Bseiso. The full list has never been released, but it included between 20 and 35 people.

The Munich terrorists were in deep hiding and difficult for assassins to reach. Mossad began assassinating saya'ans—even those who had limited involvement with the Munich operation. Across the continent, saya'ans were poisoned, gunned down on the street, or blown up in their homes or cars. Their deaths were intentionally dramatic and calculated to make an impression on other terrorists. The campaign later became known as Operation Wrath of God.

Wrath of God's Top Three Targets

In 2009, Jamal Al-Gashey was reported to be in Tunisia, a country in North Africa. In an interview for the 1999 documentary *One Day in September* he spoke of his pride at having participated in the Munich operation. He has survived several attempts on his life and remains in hiding with his wife and children. He and his wife try to give their children a normal life despite the risks of going out in public. Even though the Israeli government removed him from the hit list in 1986, his family still lives in fear.

Adnan Al-Gashey is now dead, but exactly how he died is unclear. In British author Simon Reeve's version of the story, Adnan's wife lived in terror of the assassins who stalked her husband. He had to leave the security of Lebanon to find work in one of the gulf states, where the Wrath of God hit squad killed him.

Time magazine correspondent Aaron Klein disagrees. He claims Adnan Al-Gashey actually died of heart disease in Dubai, United Arab Emirates, in 1978 or 1979.

Mohammed Safady was the man who shot the Israeli athletes at Fürstenfeldbruck military airfield. Some sources say that Mossad trapped him by tracking his family connections in Lebanon and sent assassins who killed him. However, in 2005, Safady's friend and fellow PLO member Tawfiq Tirawi claimed that Safady was "as alive as you are."[2]

Operation Spring of Youth

The 1973 Operation Spring of Youth was another Mossad mission. It was a daring covert incursion into the Arab community of Beirut, Lebanon. The goal was to kill three high-ranking PLO leaders. Although these men were not directly involved in the Munich massacre, their involvement with the PLO, which had allegedly sponsored the killings, was guilt enough for the Israelis.

The first target was the lawyer Abu Youssef. He had helped found Fatah and outranked everyone in it except Abu Iyad and Yasser Arafat. The second man marked for death was PLO Chief of Operations

Israeli Prime Minister Golda Meir in 1973

Kamel Adwan. He had commanded a militia that had carried out attacks within Israel. The last target was the PLO's spokesman, Kamal Nasser. He was almost removed from the hit list because no proof existed that he took part in terror campaigns. In the end, he stayed on the list for backing the PLO's policies.

The Israeli agents had to penetrate deep into Beirut. Instead of using Mossad assassins, this job was given to the Unit—the same elite soldiers who

Assassinated

A Palestinian extremist killed Abu Iyad and his lieutenant, Fakhri Al-Omri, in 1991. Abu Nidal was infuriated by Abu Iyad's idea that Israel could be allowed to exist side-by-side with a new Palestinian state.

In 1992, 20 years after the Munich crisis, the Israelis assassinated Abu Iyad's operations officer, Atef Bseiso.

were denied entry to Germany during the hostage crisis. To lessen suspicions, some of the shorter men dressed as women for this operation.

Agents slipped into the city by boat and split up to attack the three men in their apartments. All the targeted men were shot to death. Abu Youssef's wife and one elderly neighbor were also killed by accident. Despite a firefight that took the lives of several Lebanese police officers, the team escaped. The next day, Lebanese newspapers marveled at the women who had defeated their police with machine guns and grenades.

GERMANY TAKES RESPONSIBILITY

In 2004, Germany finally acknowledged its failure. Ankie Spitzer and Ilana Romano, leaders of the families of slain athletes, had pressured the German government for decades to release secret documents about the massacre. Finally, the documents were released, and cash settlements of a little more than $100,000 were paid to each family of the slain athletes.

*Osrat Iosef, daughter of Yossef Romano, held a picture of the
11 killed Israelis as she visited Munich in 2002.*

U.S. President Bill Clinton with Israeli Prime Minister Yitzhak Rabin, left, and PLO Chairman Yasser Arafat, right, in 1993

SEARCHING FOR PEACE

he Black September terrorists might have been successful in gaining publicity for their cause. But despite efforts to find peace, the Arab-Israeli conflict continues. Terrorism has not helped either side reach its desired result.

Terrorism after Munich

The Black September attacks at the Munich Olympics in 1972 changed the way terrorism was viewed in the world. Before then, Middle Eastern terrorism was seen as something limited to that region. Afterward, countries all over the world began to take notice of conflicts in the area.

The United States created the Cabinet Committee to Combat Terrorism in September 1972. Its goal was to learn how to both prevent and effectively respond to terrorism. After its poor handling of the hostage situation, Germany created GSG-9, an elite counterterrorism unit. Other countries followed suit.

Since 1972, countries have become better prepared to prevent attacks and to handle the aftermath. Unfortunately, as these efforts evolve, so do terrorists' methods.

Olympics after Munich

Security at the Munich Olympics was purposely limited to make people feel comfortable and safe. It proved much too limited on September 5, 1972, when the eight Black September terrorists easily snuck into the Olympic Village.

In future Olympic Games, the security at the athletes' living quarters was heightened. "Olympic villages became secure camps, diminishing the festival atmosphere, with athletes insulated from the public," said Olympics historian John MacAloon.[1] The murders at the Munich Olympics "forever changed the relationship between sport and politics," International Olympic Committee (IOC) President Jacques Rogge said at a 2004 memorial for the 11 killed Israeli athletes.[2]

Following the 1972 Olympics, the host countries also began helping future host cities prepare. All future Olympics also put in place armed security guards and a local anti-terrorism unit.

Some terrorist acts have taken place at Olympics since Munich. At the 1996 Olympics in Atlanta, Georgia, a bomb killed one person and injured more than 100 at Centennial Olympic Park. Other groups have threatened attacks or have been stopped before carrying out the attacks. Security at the Olympics became even tighter after the 9/11 terrorist attacks in the United States.

At the 2002 Salt Lake City Olympics, planes were restricted from flying above the city and sharpshooters were stationed in the mountains.

At the 2004 Athens Olympics, 70,000 armed guards patrolled the city. Unlike in Munich, where the terrorists easily climbed the wall of the Olympic Village, the wall surrounding the athletes' apartments in Athens was highly guarded by a double security fence and motion detectors. In all, security in Athens cost more than $1 billion. "There is a lot of security in the athletes' village and it makes you remember what happened," Israeli athlete Ariel Zeevi remarked at the time.[3]

At the 2008 Beijing Olympics, security included 24-hour surveillance of every Olympic venue. Plans for the 2010 Vancouver Olympics called for thousands of armed security guards, with a security budget surpassing $1.1 billion.

THE PEACE PROCESS

The Israelis and the Palestinians have taken many steps to find peace since the Munich Olympics. So far, these steps have all fallen short

Traditional Armies versus Terrorists

Someone who is reviled as a terrorist in the West might be hailed as a hero in his or her native country. The line between terrorism and conventional combat is blurry because national military forces can also cause civilian casualties. When nations at war bomb each other's cities, many of the dead are civilians. These deaths are intentional, just as deaths caused by terrorist attacks are intentional. Like conventional soldiers, terrorists do not view themselves as evil, but as committed warriors willing to give their lives for their cause.

of providing a solution. In the 1970s and through much of the 1980s, Israel remained unacceptable among its Arab neighbors, and the PLO continued to attack Israel. The Arab hostilities, including terrorism, were partly due to the territories Israel still occupied from the Six-Day War in 1967, namely the Gaza Strip, West Bank, and Old City of Jerusalem. Each of the territories had largely Palestinian populations and sought to be independent from Israel. Living conditions, especially in the Gaza Strip, were terrible. However, the hostilities stemmed from an overall refusal to accept Israel's right to exist.

The first major step toward peace in the area came

Profiling Terrorists

Psychologists study terrorists in an attempt to develop a profile, or set of characteristics, that they believe will help identify terrorists before they strike. Although characteristics continue to evolve, terrorists are often highly intelligent, well-educated people who work effectively in teams. A terrorist cell relies on those who can follow instructions or keep secrets—traits essential for carrying out plots. Because tasks and targets are divided among various cells, a terrorist who is captured cannot reveal a plan in its entirety.

Terrorists do tend to have rigid views and are not open to others' points of view. This often earns them the label of fanatics. Generally, they are not inclined to compromise and share a limited ability to see more than one solution to a problem. Unfortunately, terrorists do not have a uniform appearance that would make them easy to recognize. Racial profiling occurs when somebody is seen as a suspect simply because of his or her race.

when Egypt and Israel signed the
Treaty of 1979. In that, Egypt became
the first Arab country to recognize
Israel's right to exist. In turn, Israel
agreed to return the Sinai Peninsula,
which it had taken during the 1967
Six-Day War. Egypt was the only Arab
country to make peace with Israel
at that time, however. And Egypt
quickly fell out of favor with other
Arab nations for doing so.

In the 1980s, the international
political landscape began to change.
The Soviet Union, which had been
one of the PLO's biggest supporters,
began to weaken. Then, in 1988,
the PLO recognized Israel's right to
exist and promised to stop terrorism.
It announced it was ready to discuss
a two-state solution, whereby an
independent Palestinian state would
exist next to Israel.

The two sides secretly met in Oslo, Norway,
in 1993, to discuss the framework of a potential
two-state solution. The resulting Declaration of

**Settlements on
the West Bank**

The Palestinians hope
an eventual independent
state will be created on
the West Bank. Israeli
settlements on the West
Bank pose a major road-
block to that. Today,
approximately 280,000
Israelis live in West Bank
settlements. Where would
they go if the West Bank
became part of a new
Palestine?

In 2005, Israeli Prime
Minister Ariel Sharon
began evacuating Jew-
ish settlers from the West
Bank. The Israeli army
needed to use force to
remove some of the set-
tlers. However, in 2009,
Israelis still occupied
approximately 120 settle-
ments in the West Bank
and more were being
built.

Principles reiterated the PLO's recognition of Israel and its vow to end violence against Israel. Israel in turn acknowledged the PLO as the voice for the Palestinian people. Israel also promised to withdraw from the West Bank and the Gaza Strip and to consider an independent Palestinian state on those lands. One year later, in 1994, Israel signed a peace treaty with its neighbor, Jordan.

In 2000, U.S. President Bill Clinton invited Yasser Arafat from the PLO and Israeli Prime Minister Ehud Barak to discuss a permanent solution. At the meetings, Barak is said to have offered an independent Palestinian state. Arafat, however, had said before the meetings that he would only accept full sovereignty, or independence from Israel. He rejected Barak's offer, and the conflict continued.

Operation Defensive Shield

In 2002, Israel launched Operation Defensive Shield to damage the infrastructure that supported Palestinian terrorism. Among the targets in Israel's attack were "terrorist facilities and explosives, laboratories, weapons production factories and secret installations," Israeli Prime Minister Ariel Sharon said in a speech.[4]

INTO A NEW MILLENNIUM

The peace process began breaking down after the failed negotiations with Clinton, and violence between the two sides began escalating. By 2002, Israel decided the only way to

stop Palestinian terrorism was to initiate Operation
Defensive Shield, in which it attacked Palestinian
terrorism infrastructure. Soon after, Israel began
reclaiming cities in the West Bank that it had
returned to the Palestinians in the 1990s. It also
began building a wall between Israel and the West
Bank.

Hopes rose again in 2003 when an international
coalition including the United States proposed a
"roadmap" for peace. The two sides tried again
in 2005 with the signing of an Israeli-Palestinian
truce. But neither initiative brought lasting peace.

The peace process suffered a major setback in
2006 when Hamas, a militant group dedicated
to creating a Palestinian state and eliminating
Israel, gained a majority in the new Palestinian
government and later took control over the Gaza
Strip. Palestinian militants continued launching
rocket attacks into Israel from Gaza, and the new
Palestinian government showed unwillingness to
discuss peace.

Tensions between the two sides flared up again
at the end of 2008. Hamas militants sent rockets
from Gaza into Israel. In response, Israel launched
a large-scale attack on the Gaza Strip. More than

1,300 people, the vast majority Palestinians, were killed. Israel declared a cease-fire on January 17, 2009. Hamas followed with a cease-fire the next day.

JUSTICE, THEN PEACE

The disputes over this land go back thousands of years. No one knows how long it will be until the Palestinians have an independent state, if they ever do. The issues that have prompted terrorist acts such as those at the 1972 Munich Olympics are incredibly complex. What are the rights of Israelis? What are the rights of Palestinians? What is the best way to balance these rights and find a fair solution?

The Black September terrorists at the Munich Olympics did not achieve their ultimate goal, which was to eliminate the State of Israel. Yet, their failure did not discourage others. Militants on both sides of the conflict continued to commit terrorist acts. When it comes to the Arab-Israeli conflict, "justice" might be difficult to define. However, the slow and challenging work of achieving justice in the Middle East is the world's only hope for stopping terrorism between the region's long-standing enemies. —

A Palestinian flag waved above the rubble after Israeli attacks
in Gaza during January 2009.

TIMELINE

1800–1500 BCE	132–135 BCE	1917
Hebrew tribes settle Canaan. Arabic tribes are also present in the region.	Middle Eastern Jews scatter throughout Europe after their unsuccessful revolt against the Romans.	In the Balfour Declaration, Britain supports the creation of a Jewish nation in Palestine.

1945	1947	1948
On May 8, the Holocaust comes to an end with the Allied victory in World War II.	The United Nations unsuccessfully attempts to divide Palestine into a Jewish state and an Arab state in November.	The Israeli-Arab war breaks out and British forces leave Palestine.

1918	1933–1945	1936
An influx of Jews immigrates to Palestine after World War I, hoping to build a homeland there.	The Nazis kill approximately 6 million Jews as well as members of other persecuted groups in the Holocaust.	Hitler tries to use the Berlin Olympics to prove Aryan superiority; some Jews are prevented from competing.

1948	1948	ca. 1958
On April 9, in the Deir Yassin massacre, Jewish guerillas attack an Arab village and execute more than 100 people.	The nation of Israel is founded on May 14, displacing 700,000 Palestinians to refugee camps.	Yasser Arafat founds the revolutionary organization Fatah.

TIMELINE

1964	1970	1972
The Palestine Liberation Organization (PLO) is founded.	In September, Jordan's King Hussein launches attacks against Palestinian fedayeen.	Black September begins assassinating Arabs who collaborated with Israel and attacking businesses with Israeli interests.

1972	1987	1993
After a hijacking, Germans release the Munich terrorists on October 29. Israel sends assassins after them.	Hamas, one of the major political parties in the PLO, is founded.	The PLO recognizes Israel and vows to end violence against the country in the Declaration of Principles.

1972

In May, Black September attempts to hijack a plane bound for Tel Aviv, Israel, but is prevented by Israeli troops.

1972

Black September terrorists take Israeli athletes hostage at the Munich Olympics on September 5.

1972

The United States creates the Cabinet Committee to Combat Terrorism in September.

1994

The Nobel Peace Prize is awarded to Arafat, Rabin, and Peres for efforts to create peace in the Middle East.

2000

Israel and the PLO discuss a permanent solution with U.S. President Bill Clinton but fail to reach an agreement.

2008

Israel responds to Hamas rockets by attacking the Gaza Strip. Hundreds are killed, mostly Palestinians.

Essential Facts

Date of Event

September 5–6, 1972

Place of Event

Munich, West Germany

Key Players

- ❖ Black September terrorist organization
- ❖ Israeli Olympic delegation
- ❖ Muhammad Massalha (Issa), terrorist leader
- ❖ Hans-Dietrich Genscher, German interior minister
- ❖ Walther Tröger, Olympic Village mayor
- ❖ Hans-Jochen Vogel, Munich mayor

Highlights of Event

❖ On September 5, 1972, Black September terrorists took
  11 members of the Israeli delegation hostage at the Munich
  Olympics.

❖ The terrorists demanded the release of 234 prisoners in Israel
  and two in Germany.

❖ Later that day, the terrorists and their hostages were transported
  to Fürstenfeldbruck military airfield, where all of the Israelis and
  all but three of the terrorists died.

❖ On October 29, 1972, Black September hijacked a Lufthansa
  Boeing 727 and picked up the three surviving terrorists,
  returning them to friendly Arab countries.

❖ Israel launched Operation Wrath of God and Operation Spring
  of Youth to seek revenge on those involved with the Munich
  Olympics massacre.

Quotes

"If we should give in, then no Israeli anywhere in the world will feel
that his life is safe. It's blackmail of the worst kind."—*Golda Meir,
Israeli prime minister*

"We are dead anyway, either we will be killed here, or if we go out
and give up without having hostages . . . we will be killed where we
go."—*Issa, lead terrorist in Munich attack*

ADDITIONAL RESOURCES

SELECT BIBLIOGRAPHY

Bolz, Frank, Kenneth J. Dudonis, and David P. Schulz. *The Counterterrorism Handbook: Tactics, Procedures, and Techniques.* New York, NY: CRC Press, 2005.

Jewish Virtual Library. 2009. 23 Mar. 2009 <http://www.jewishvirtuallibrary.org>.

Klein, Aaron. *Striking Back.* New York, NY: Random House, 2005.

"Life in a Palestinian Refugee Camp" *Al Awda: The Palestinian Right to Return Coalition.* 2009. 23 Mar. 2009 <http://www.al-awda.org/index.html>.

Reeve, Simon. *One Day in September.* New York, NY: Arcade Publishing, 2000.

FURTHER READING

Levitas, Mitchel, ed. *The New York Times: A Nation Challenged, Young Reader's Edition.* New York, NY: Callaway Scholastic Nonfiction, 2002.

Meltzer, Milton. *The Day the Sky Fell: A History of Terrorism.* New York, NY: Random House Books for Young Readers, 2002.

WEB LINKS

To learn more about the terrorist attacks at the Munich Olympics, visit ABDO Publishing Company online at **www.abdopublishing.com**. Web sites about the terrorist attacks at the Munich Olympics are featured on our Book Links page. These links are routinely monitored and updated to provide the most current information available.

PLACES TO VISIT

Museum of Tolerance
9786 West Pico Boulevard, Los Angeles, CA 90035
310-553-8403
www.museumoftolerance.com
The museum challenges its visitors to confront intolerance through interactive exhibits, arts, and lectures.

New York Tolerance Center
226 East 42nd Street, New York, NY 10017
212-697-1314
www.museumoftolerance.com/site/c.juLVJ8MRKtH/
b.1353929/k.6543/New_York_Tolerance_Center.htm
The center offers daylong educational and experiential sessions with workshops, exhibits, and videos to promote tolerance and cooperation.

The U.S. Holocaust Memorial Museum
100 Raoul Wallenberg Place, Washington, DC 20024-2126
202-488-0400
www.ushmm.org
The museum acts as a memorial to the Holocaust while also working to prevent anything similar from ever happening again.

GLOSSARY

anti-Semitism
A dislike for and prejudice against Jewish people.

assassin
A person who commits a murder, usually with a political motive.

casualties
People injured or killed in an attack or event.

cell
A small group of people serving as a part of a larger political movement.

charisma
Personal charm or attractiveness that makes an individual influential.

diaspora
The dispersal of a population sharing a common ethnic identity from their home territory to many remote locations.

fundamentalism
A traditionalist and anti-modernist movement within a religion, requiring strict adherence to the basic principles of the religion.

genocide
The systematic killing of a particular racial or cultural group.

hijack
The seizure of a vehicle in transit, either to rob it, take hostages, or divert it to an alternate destination.

incompetence
Not doing a good job; showing a lack of skill or aptitude.

martyr
> A person who has died because of his or her faith.

militant
> A person or organization displaying aggressive and violent behavior in pursuit of a political cause.

negotiation
> Conferring with others in order to come to terms or reach an agreement.

retaliation
> A violent response that seeks revenge for an attack or injustice.

surveillance
> The passive gathering of information about someone or something by monitoring behavior, events, and actions.

swastika
> The official emblem of the Nazi Party and the Third Reich; a cross with the arms bent at right angles in a clockwise direction.

tactical
> Relating to tactics, the branch of military science dealing with detailed maneuvers to achieve objectives set by strategy.

terrorism
> The illegal use of force or violence against civilians or property for purposes of intimidation, coercion, or ransom.

SOURCE NOTES

Chapter 1. "The Games of Peace and Joy"
1. Mike Morrison. "Jesse Owens: Track Star Jesse Owens Defiantly Bucks Hitler" *Memorable Olympics Moments*. Infoplease. 2007. 23 Mar. 2009 <http://www.infoplease.com/spot/summer-olympics-jesse-owens.html>.
2. Clark McCauley. "The Psychology of Terrorism." *Social Science Research Council*. 23 Mar. 2009 <http://www.ssrc.org/sept11/essays/mccauley.htm>.

Chapter 2. Ancient Roots of a Modern War
None.

Chapter 3. Israeli Statehood
1. *The Living Bible Paraphrased*. Wheaton, IL: Tyndale House Publishers, 1971. 12.
2. "The Balfour Declaration." *BBC*. 29 Nov. 2001. 4 Mar. 2009 <http://news.bbc.co.uk/2/hi/in_depth/middle_east/israel_and_the_palestinians/key_documents/1682961.stm>.

Chapter 4. Before Munich

1. Aaron Klein. *Striking Back.* New York: Random House, 2005. 31.

Chapter 5. Taking Hostages

1. Simon Reeve. *One Day in September.* New York: Arcade Publishing, 2000. 2.
2. Ibid. 4.
3. Ibid. 8.
4. Ibid. xii.
5. Ibid. 7.
6. Ibid. 8.

Chapter 6. Broken Promises, Shattered Lives

1. Aaron Klein. *Striking Back.* New York: Random House, 2005. 58.
2. Simon Reeve. *One Day in September.* New York: Arcade Publishing, 2000. 62.
3. Ibid. 60.

Source Notes Continued

Chapter 7. The Bitter End
1. Aaron Klein. *Striking Back.* New York: Random House, 2005. 44.
2. Simon Reeve. *One Day in September.* New York: Arcade Publishing, 2000. 89.
3. Aaron Klein. *Striking Back.* New York: Random House, 2005. 69.
4. Ibid. 80.
5. Simon Reeve. *One Day in September.* New York: Arcade Publishing, 2000. 135.

Chapter 8. Vengeance
1. Aaron Klein. *Striking Back*. New York: Random House, 2005. 138.
2. Lisa Beyer. "The Myths and Reality of Munich." *Time.* 5 Dec. 2005. 23 Mar. 2009 <http://www.time.com/time/magazine/article/0,9171,1137646,00.html>.

Chapter 9. Searching for Peace
1. Dan Gilgoff. "The Meaning of Munich." *U.S. News and World Report.* 6 June, 2004. 5 May, 2009 <http://www.usnews.com/usnews/culture/articles/040614/14olympics.b.htm>.
2. Matthew Davis. "Athens 2004 Remembers Munich 1972." BBC. Aug. 20, 2004. May 5, 2009. <http://news.bbc.co.uk/2/hi/europe/3581866.stm>.
3. Ibid.
4. Bernard Reich. "A Brief History of Israel. Second Edition." New York: Checkmark Books, 2008. 231.

INDEX

INDEX CONTINUED

About the Author

Courtney Farrell taught biology and microbiology for ten years at Front Range Community College in Colorado, but she is now a full-time writer. She has contributed to college-level biology textbooks and has authored several books for young people on social issues and historical events. Farrell has a Master of Science in Zoology and is interested in conservation and sustainability issues. She lives with her husband and sons on a ranch in the mountains of Colorado.

Photo Credits

Kurt Strumpf/AP Images, cover; AP Images, 6, 11, 15, 23, 24, 32, 49, 51, 52, 56, 61, 62, 65, 70, 73, 74, 97 (top), 97 (bottom), 99 (top); Peter Dejong/AP Images, 16, 96; Adel Hana/AP Images, 27; Red Line Editorial, 31; Jerome Delay/AP Images, 37; Family Handout Via Alexandra Boulat/VII/AP Images, 41; Jan Pitman/AP Images, 42; Giuseppe Anastasi/AP Images, 83; Jan Pitman/AP Images, 85; Ron Edmonds/AP Images, 86, 99 (bottom, left); Hatem Moussa/AP Images, 95, 99 (bottom, right)